**W9-CKL-919**

# POEMS FOR AUTUMN

## Selected by
## Robert Hull

## Illustrated by
## Annabel Spenceley

STECK-VAUGHN
L I B R A R Y
A Division of Steck-Vaughn Company

*Austin, Texas*

# Seasonal Poetry

## Poems for Autumn
## Poems for Spring
## Poems for Summer
## Poems for Winter

Series editor: Catherine Ellis
Designer: Ross George

© **Copyright this edition 1991,
Steck-Vaughn Co.**

### Library of Congress Cataloging in Publication Data

Poems for autumn / selected by Robert Hull : illustrated by Annabel
Spenceley
   p. cm. — (Seasonal poetry)
   Includes index.
   Summary: An anthology of poems reflecting autumn by such authors
as Thomas Hardy, Theodore Roethke, and Maurice Sendak.
   ISBN 0-8114-7800-9
   1. Autumn — Juvenile poetry. 2. Children's poetry. 3. Poetry —
Collections.  4.  English poetry — Translations from foreign
languages. [1. Autumn — Poetry.  2. Poetry — Collections.]
I. Hull, Robert.  II. Spenceley, Annabel. ill.  III. Series.
PN6109.97.P634 1991
808.81'933 — dc20                                    90-20590
                                                       CIP AC

## Picture Acknowledgments

The publishers would like to thank the
following for allowing their illustrations to be
reproduced in this book: Celtic Picture
Agency 41; Bruce Coleman *Cover*, (Hans
Reinhard) 5, (Hans Reinhard) 21, (Roger
Wilmshurst) 33, (John Shaw) 45; Eric & David
Hosking (George Hyde) 11; Frank Lane
Picture Agency (R Van Nostrand) 7, (M.
Nimmo) 17, (Peggy Heard) 29, (J. Bastable)
42; Topham Picture Library (Windridge) 13,
14, 18, 26, 38; Zefa (Palmer) 23, (Damm) 24,
31, 34, 37.

Typeset by Nicola Taylor, Wayland
Printed in Italy by G. Canale & C.S.p.A.
Bound in the United States
   2   3   4   5   Ca   95   94   93

## Acknowledgments

For permission to reprint copyright material
the publishers gratefully acknowledge the
following: Faber & Faber Ltd for "October
Nights in My Cabin" from *Snowman Sniffles*
by N. M. Bodecker; the Estate of Robert Frost,
E. Connery Lathem and Jonathan Cape Ltd
for "Gathering Leaves" from *The Collected
Poems of Robert Frost* edited by Edward
Connery Lathem; Faber & Faber Ltd for
"There Came a Day" from *Season Songs* by
Ted Hughes; the author and the Bodley Head
for "Apple Song" from *The Spitfire on the
Northern Line* by Brian Jones; Chatto &
Windus/The Hogarth Press for "Rowan
Berry" from *Collected Poems* by Norman
MacCaig; Faber & Faber Ltd for "The Coming
of the Cold" from the *Collected Poems* of
Theodore Roethke; Collins Publishers for
"October" from *Chicken Soup with Rice* by
Maurice Sendak; reprinted with permission
of Macmillan Publishing Company,
"Something Told the Wild Geese", © 1934
Macmillan renewed 1967 by Arthur S.
Pederson; Penguin Books for the two Haiku
poems by Masaoka Shiki trans. by Bownas
and Thwaite from *Penguin Book of Japanese
Verse*; Harcourt Brace Jovanovich for
"Crabapples" and "Theme in Yellow" by Carl
Sandburg; Doubleday for "The Coming of
the Cold" from *Collected Poems of Theodore
Roethke*; Wes Magee for "Tracey's Tree";
Cynthia Mitchell for "O Witches and
Wizards"; Matt Simpson for "Autumn
Haiku"; for "Witch's Broom Notes" from *One
at a Time* by David McCord, copyright ©
1965, 1966, 1974 by David McCord. By
permission of Little, Brown and Company.
"Proud Torsos" from *Good Morning,
America*, copyright 1928 and renewed 1956
by Carl Sandburg, reprinted by permission of
Harcourt Brace Jovanovich, Inc.

While every effort has been made to secure
permission, in some cases it has proved
impossible to trace the copyright holders.
The publishers apologize for this apparent
negligence.

# Contents

# Introduction

What does autumn make you think of? Blackberrying? Hallowe'en? Leaves falling? Coming in earlier because it gets dark sooner? Probably all of these things. And it means things like that to poets, too. It means feeling the sun getting chillier, sweeping leaves, going to harvest festivals, watching birds gobbling berries.

Poets do a lot of noticing. They notice insects getting slower. They notice the orchard trees "sagging." They STOP to look hard at things – until they see something they hadn't seen before. Have you ever played the game of staring at something until it reminds you of something else? You look hard at a tree-trunk and it becomes the skin of a dinosaur, or at a cauliflower until it reminds you of. . .? That's always happening to poets.

That's how you can write autumn poems. Go outside to have a look at what's going on, get some horse chestnuts, pick some apples and blackberries, rake up some leaves. Write. Read these poems again.

# Something Told the Wild Geese

Something told the wild geese
   It was time to go.
Though the fields lay golden
   Something whispered — "Snow."
Leaves were green and stirring,
   Berries, luster-glossed,
But beneath warm feathers
   Something cautioned — "Frost."
All the sagging orchards
   Steamed with amber spice,
But each wild breast stiffened
   At remembered ice.
Something told the wild geese
   It was time to fly —
Summer sun was on their wings,
   Winter in their cry.

**RACHEL FIELD**

# *There Came a Day*

There came a day that caught the summer
Wrung its neck
Plucked it
And ate it.

Now what shall I do with the trees?
The day said, the day said.
Strip them bare, strip them bare.
Let's see what is really there.

And what shall I do with the sun?
The day said, the day said.
Roll him away till he's cold and small.
He'll come back rested if he comes back at all.

And what shall I do with the birds?
The day said, the day said.
The birds I've frightened, let them flit,
I'll hang out pork for the brave tomtit.

*tomtit* – a small bird that moves quickly

And what shall I do with the seed?
The day said, the day said.
Bury it deep, see what it's worth.
See if it can stand the earth.

What shall I do with the people?
The day said, the day said.
Stuff them with apple and blackberry pie –
They'll love me then till the day they die.

There came this day and he was autumn.
His mouth was wide
And red as a sunset.
His tail was an icicle.

**TED HUGHES**

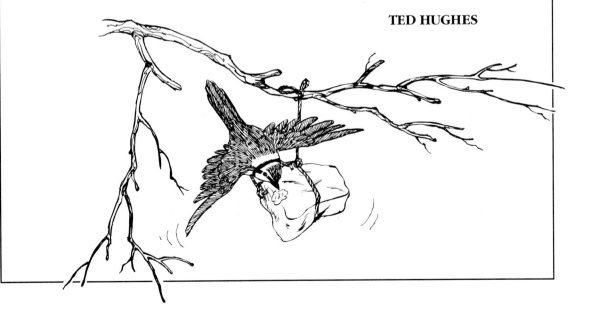

# *About Caterpillars*

What about caterpillars?
Where do they crawl
when the stars say, "Frost,"
and the leaves say, "Fall?"

Some go to sleep
in a white silk case
when the winds say, "Blow!"
and the clouds say, "Race!"

Some sleep in bags
of woven brown
or curl in a ball
when the year says, "Frown."

None has the least
little urge to know
what the world is like
when the sky says, "Snow."

**AILEEN FISHER**

# *Bumble Bee*

I am a bumble bee,
think kindly thoughts of me,
I filled my summer mornings
 with my humming.

Now days are growing short
and I suppose I ought
to stop this evening mumble
 in the clover;

but when I think it's done,
the hum goes on and on,
for no-one will believe
 that winter's coming;

when stillness should begin,
small songs keep dropping in
like raindrops from the trees
 when rain is over.

**N. M. BODECKER**

13

# *Apple Song*

I am an apple
I swing on the tree
I have a sharpness
At the heart of me

And no sun at noonday
Brutal with heat
Can utterly tame me
And render me sweet

Don't eat me on picnics
At height of midsummer
With lettuce and radish
Tomatoes, cucumber

When your body is tanned
And your mind thick as cream
And all life a languorous
Strawberry dream

And when Autumn is stirred
By a spoon of a wind
And the clothes you are wearing
Seem suddenly thinned

And your walk through the orchard
Is vaguely beset
By currents of feeling –
Nostalgia, regret,

And you need an assurance
That December and June
Can be blended together,
Pluck me down. Eat me then.

**BRIAN JONES**

**15**

*languorous* - slow moving, without any energy

# *Rowan Berry*

I'm at ease in my crimson cluster.
The tree blazes
with clusters of cousins –
my cluster's the main one and I
am the important berry in it.

Tomorrow, or tomorrow's tomorrow,
a flock of fieldfares
will gobble our whole generation.

I'm not troubled. My seed
will be shamelessly dropped
somewhere. And in the next years
after next year, I'll be a tree
swaying and swinging
with a genealogy of berries. I'll be
that fine thing, an ancestor.
I'll spread out my branches
for the guzzling fieldfares.

**NORMAN MacCAIG**

**16**

*rowan berry* - the fruit of the rowan tree, which is from the rose family.
*fieldfare* - a medium-sized bird, a thrush.

# Tracey's Tree

Last year it was not there,
the sapling with purplish leaves
planted in our school grounds with care.
It's Tracey's tree, my friend who died,
and last year it was not there.

Tracey, the girl with long black hair
who, out playing one day, ran
across a main road for a dare.
The lorry struck her. Now a tree grows
and last year it was not there.

Through the classroom window I stare
and watch the sapling sway.
Soon its branches will stand bare.
It wears a forlorn and lonely look
and last year it was not there.

October's chill is in the air
and cold rain distorts my view.
I feel a sadness that's hard to bear.
The tree blurs, as if I've been crying,
and last year it was not there.

**WES MAGEE**

19

# *Theme in Yellow*

I spot the hills
With yellow balls in autumn.
I light the prairie cornfields
Orange and tawny gold clusters
And I am called pumpkins.
On the last of October
When dusk is fallen
Children join hands
And circle round me
Singing ghost songs
And love to the harvest moon;
I am a jack-o'-lantern
With terrible teeth
And the children know
I am fooling.

**CARL SANDBURG**

# Witch's Broom Notes

On Halloween, what bothers some
About these witches is, how come
In sailing through the air like bats
They never seem to lose their hats?

Hitchhiking owls, as we have seen,
Ride nicely on this queer machine.
Black cats have been reported too;
Which isn't possible or true.

Another thing: if brooms can fly,
Do witches keep them handy–by
To sweep the kitchen floor with, say?
Or do they have them locked away
For private passage through the sky?

All witches ride well forward, aim
Their broomstick handles, make no claim
For anything like a magic jet.
Who knows a witch's air speed yet?

**DAVID McCORD**

23

# *October Nights in My Cabin*

Acorns drop
on my roof
all night,
each with a hard
little:
"Plonk!"

Raindrops drum
on my roof
all-right
like fingertips
over
my bunk.

Wild geese pass over
my roof
in flight,
the old, grey
travelers
honk!

There's a patter of feet
on my roof
that might
be a squirrel,
or chipmunk,
or skunk. . .

and acorns keep dropping
– or aren't they
*quite*
acorns, the things
that go:
"Bonk!"

but peanuts dropped
in the pale moonlight
from a fumble-nose
elephant's
trunk?

**N. M. BODECKER**

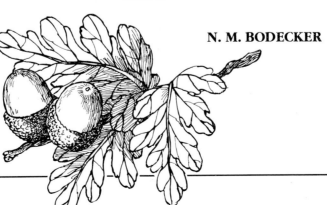

# *Thanksgiving Day*

Thanks to the few who first came here
when the forests ran with turkey and deer.
Thanks to all those who cleared a way
through a hard land so we feast today.
Thanks to all laborers, every last one
working a passage in storm and sun.
Thanks to each bus-driver, teacher, nurse,
steel-worker, check-out girl, writer of verse.
Thanks to the Presidents we all remember
and the folks we'll forget by next November.
Thanks to our families, this one first,
who've brought us up to be ... not the worst ...
and earned the food that's spread on the table.
(We promise to eat no more than we're able,
even those sugary ginger-bread men
that look so good we could eat all ten.)
Thanks for grandmother's pumpkin pie,
and the laughing look in grandfather's eye.
Thanks for pears and plums and apples,
and all the lights in roadside chapels.
Thanks for sunlight and thanks for air.
Thanks to the earth for being there.
Thanks for brothers and sisters and friends
and the warmth of home when a day ends.

**TRISH COLBI EMET**

27

# *Crabapples*

Sweeten these bitter wild crabapples, Illinois
October sun. The roots here came from the
wilderness, came before man came here. They
are bitter as the wild is bitter.

Give these crabapples your softening gold,
October sun, go through to the white wet
seeds inside and soften them black. Make
these bitter apples sweet. They want you, sun.

The drop and the fall, the drop and the fall,
the apples leaving the branches for the black
earth under, they know you from last year,
the year before last year, October sun.

**CARL SANDBURG**

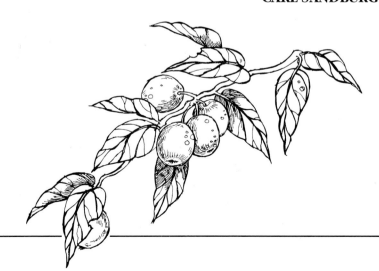

# *October*

In October
I'll be host
to witches, goblins
and a ghost.
I'll serve them
chicken soup
on toast.
Whoopy once
whoopy twice
whoopy chicken soup
with rice.

**MAURICE SENDAK**

# *Proud Torsos*

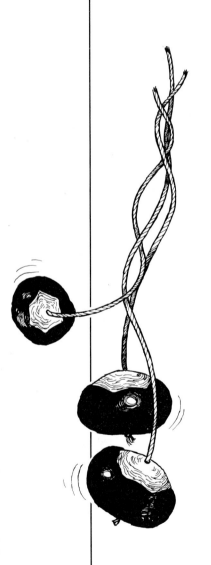

Just before the high time of autumn
Comes with the crush of its touch,
And the leaves fall, the leaves one by one,
The leaves by a full darkening sky fall.
The trees look proud, the horse chestnut
Stands with a gathered pride, the ivies
Are gathered around the stumps.
The ivies are woven thick with a green coat
Covering the stumps.  Yes, the trees
Look proud now, it is the big time
Have they not all had summer?
Didn't they all flimmer with faint
Lines of green in the spring,
A thin green mist as if it might
Be air or it might be new green leaves?
So, the first weeks of September are on
and each tree stands with a murmur,
"I stand here with a count of one more year,
 One more number, one more ring in my torso."
Two weeks, five, six weeks, and the trees
Will be standing ... stripped ... gaunt ...
The leaves gone ... the coat of green gone ...
And they will be proud but no longer
With gathered pride of the days
In the high time.

**CARL SANDBURG**

# *Gathering Leaves*

Spades take up leaves
No better than spoons,
And bags full of leaves
Are light as balloons.

I make a great noise
Of rustling all day
Like rabbit and deer
Running away.

But the mountains I raise
Elude my embrace,
Flowing over my arms
And into my face.

I may load and unload
Again and again
Till I fill the whole shed,
And what have I then?

Next to nothing for weight,
And since they grew duller
From contact with earth,
Next to nothing for color.

Next to nothing for use.
But a crop is a crop,
And who's to say where
The harvest shall stop?

**ROBERT FROST**

# *O Witches and Wizards*

O witches and wizards, where have you been?
    We've been to a party for old Hallowe'en.

A Hallowe'en party! O what did you eat?
    Spiced turnip lanterns and hot cauldron treat.

And after the eating what games did you play?
    Old Spells, Hokey-Pokey, and Scare-Them-Away.

And after the game did you all dance together?
    We danced like the North wind in rough, stormy
        weather.

O witches and wizards, what else did you do?
    *Ah, that is our secret. We cannot tell you.*

**CYNTHIA MITCHELL**

37

# *The Roof Whirled Away by Winds*

In the eighth moon of autumn, the wind howling viciously,
Three layers of thatch were whirled away from my roof.
The thatch flying over the river sprinkled the embankment
And some of it was entangled in the treetops,
And some whirled away and sank in the marshlands.
A swarm of small boys from South Village laughing at me because
    I am old and feeble.
They know they can rob me even in my face.
What effrontery! Stealing my thatch, taking it to the bamboo
    grove.
With parched lips and tongue I screamed at them – it was no
    use –
And so I came back sighing to my old place.
Then the wind fell and the clouds were inky black,
The autumn sky a web of darkness, stretching toward the dusk,
And my old cotton quilt was as cold as iron,
And my darling son tossed in his sleep, bare feet tearing
    through the blanket,
And the rain dripped through the roof, and there was no dry
    place on the bed.
Like strings of wax the rain fell, unending.
After all these disasters of war, I have had little sleep or rest.
When will this long night of drizzle come to an end?

**TU FU**

*effrontery* - boldness with no shame

# A Sheep Fair

The day arrives of the autumn fair,
    And torrents fall,
Though sheep in throngs are gathered there,
    Ten thousand all,
Sodden, with hurdles round them reared:
And, lot by lot, the pens are cleared,
And the auctioneer wrings out his beard,
And wipes his book, bedrenched and smeared,
And rakes the rain from his face with the edge of his hand,
    As torrents fall.

The wool of the ewes is like a sponge
    With the daylong rain:
Jammed tight, to turn, or lie, or lunge,
    They strive in vain.
Their horns are as soft as finger-nails,
Their shepherds reek against the rails,
The tied dogs soak with tucked-in tails,
The buyers' hat-brims fill like pails,
Which spill small cascades when they shift their stand
    In the daylong rain.

**THOMAS HARDY**

# *Autumn Haiku*

This Way Winter! say
a robin's arrow-tracks on
the garden's first snow.

**MATT SIMPSON**

He washes his horse
With the setting sun
In the autumn sea.

**MASAOKA SHIKI**

A snake falls
From the high stone wall:
Fierce autumn gale.

**MASAOKA SHIKI**

# The Coming of the Cold

The ribs of leaves lie in the dust,
The beak of frost has picked the bough,
The briar bears its thorn, and drought
Has left its ravage on the field.
The season's wreckage lies about,
Late autumn fruit is rotted now.
All shade is lean, the antic branch
Jerks skyward at the touch of wind,
Dense trees no longer hold the light,
The hedge and orchard grove are thinned.
The dank bark dries beneath the sun,
The last of harvesting is done.
All things are brought to barn and fold
The oak leaves strain to be unbound,
The sky turns dark, the year grows old,
The buds draw in before the cold.

**THEODORE ROETHKE**

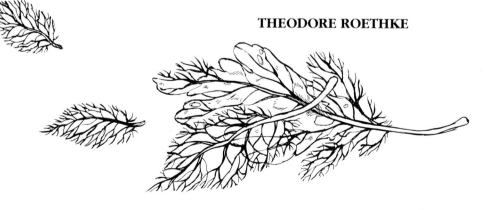

*antic* - playful          *ravage* - result of the damage from something destructive

# Biographies

**N. M. Bodecker** was born in Denmark, and now lives in the U.S. He spent his early life painting and drawing, then started to write at about twenty. He has three sons and lives in New Hampshire in an old haunted house.

**Rachel Field** (1894–1942) was an American writer. She was born in New York, then lived in Massachusetts. She wrote lots of children's poetry and stories, and novels for adults.

**Aileen Fisher** is best known for *In the Woods, in the Meadow, in the Sky,* a poetry collection published in 1965.

**Robert Frost** (1874–1963) is one of the most famous American poets of this century. He was born in California, and later lived on a farm in New Hampshire. Although he did not write especially for children, many of his poems are children's favorites.

**Tu Fu** is one of the most famous Chinese poets. He lived more than a thousand years ago, from AD 712 to 770, and wrote hundreds of poems.

**Thomas Hardy** (1840–1928) was a famous novelist and poet, who lived nearly all his long life in Dorset. He is one of the greatest English poets.

**Ted Hughes** was born in Yorkshire, England. In 1984 he was made Poet Laureate. He has written many books for adults and for children. One of the best known for children is *Season Songs.*

**Brian Jones** was born in London, and now lives in Kent. He has published books of poems for children and adults, and has received many awards.

**Norman MacCaig** was born in 1910 in Edinburgh. He writes a great deal about Scotland, and has published many collections of poetry.

**Wes Magee** lives in Yorkshire, England. He is a full-time writer who started writing for adults and went on to write books for children. A recent one is *Morning Break,* voted one of the best children's books of 1989.

**David McCord** an American poet, was born in 1897. He has written many books about many things – art, education, medicine and history – but he is best known for his light verse, and especially his poems for children.

**Cynthia Mitchell** lives in Yorkshire, England, where she used to be deputy head of an infants' school. She has written three books of verse for children. She visits schools with her poems, and likes to get children to skip and dance and be active with her poems, as you might guess from the title of one book: *Hopalong Happily*.

**Theodore Roethke** (1908–1963) was born in Saginaw, Michigan. After leaving Chicago he taught English at several colleges in the U.S. His poems for children are in a book called *I Am! Says the Lamb!*

**Carl Sandburg** (1878–1967) was an American writer. He wrote many stories and poems for children. They are collected in a beautiful book called *The Sandburg Treasury*.

**Maurice Sendak** is best known as an illustrator of many children's books, such as the famous *Where the Wild Things Are*, voted the best picture book of 1963 in the U.S. He was born in Brooklyn in 1928, and started making books with his brother Jack when they were both quite young.

**Masaoka Shiki** (1867–1902) was a Japanese writer of haiku. Haiku are three-line poems which have been popular in Japan for many centuries. Shiki used to advise his pupils to "be natural" and try for "real pictures" when writing poetry.

**Matt Simpson** started writing for children only fairly recently. His latest book of poems for adults is called *An Elegy for the Galosherman*. He lives in Liverpool, England, where he lectures in English, and visits schools to read his poetry.

# Index of First Lines

First published in 1990 by
Wayland (Publishers) Ltd

© Copyright 1990 Wayland
(Publishers) Ltd